Environmental Fitness and Resilience

A Review of Relevant Constructs, Measures, and Links to Well-Being

Regina A. Shih, Sarah O. Meadows, John Mendeloff, Kirby Bowling

RAND Project AIR FORCE

Prepared for the United States Air Force
Approved for public release; distribution unlimited

For more information on this publication, visit www.rand.org/t/RR101

Library of Congress Cataloging-in-Publication Data is available for this publication.

ISBN: 978-0-8330-9099-7

Published by the RAND Corporation, Santa Monica, Calif.
© Copyright 2015 RAND Corporation

RAND® is a registered trademark.

Support RAND
Make a tax-deductible charitable contribution at
www.rand.org/giving/contribute

www.rand.org

Preface

U.S. military personnel have been engaged in operations in Central Asia and the Middle East for the past decade. Members of the armed forces also deploy to other regions of the world. Many aspects of deployments have the potential to contribute to individual stress, such as uncertainty about deployment time lines; culture shock in theater; fear of or confrontation with death or physical injury; environmental challenges, such as extreme climates and geographical features; austere living conditions; separation from friends and family members; and reintegration after deployment. Service members and their families also manage other military-related stressors, such as frequent relocations, long work hours, and the additional family separations associated with unaccompanied tours and domestic training exercises. Some service members and their families may cope well or even thrive as they overcome adversity and accomplish challenging tasks. However, some may suffer negative consequences as a result of military-related stressors, such as physical injury, including traumatic brain injury; depression, anxiety, or other mood disorders; post-traumatic stress disorder; spiritual crises; substance abuse; family dysfunction; marital problems and dissolutions; social isolation; and, in extreme cases, even suicide or suicide attempts. With the aim of preventing such deleterious outcomes rather than simply responding to them, the study of resilience is of paramount importance.

The Air Force offices of Airman and Family Services (AF/A1S), the Surgeon General (AF/SG), and the Deputy Assistant Secretary of the Air Force for Force Management Integration (SAF/MRM) asked the RAND Corporation to help the Air Force develop its programs to promote resiliency among military and civilian Air Force personnel and their families. This report is one in a series of nine reports that resulted from that research effort.

The overarching report, *Airman and Family Resilience: Lessons from the Scientific Literature* (Meadows, Miller, and Robson, 2015), provides an introduction to resilience concepts and research, documents established and emerging Air Force resiliency efforts, and reviews Air Force metrics for tracking the resiliency of Air Force personnel and their families. It also provides recommendations to support the development of resilience initiatives across the Air Force. We use the term *resilience* to refer to the ability to withstand, recover from, and grow in the face of stressors and *fitness*, which is related, as a "state of adaptation in balance with the conditions at hand" (Mullen, 2010).

Accompanying that overarching report are eight supplemental reports that outline the constructs, metrics, and influential factors relevant to resiliency across the eight domains of Total Force Fitness:

- medical
- nutritional
- environmental

- physical
- social
- spiritual
- behavioral
- psychological.

These supplemental reports are not intended to be a comprehensive review of the entire literature within a domain. Rather, they focus on studies that consider the stress-buffering aspects of each domain, regardless of whether the term *resilience* is specifically used. This expanded the scope of the reviews to include a broader range of applicable studies and also allowed for terminology differences that occur across different disciplines (e.g., stress management, hardiness).

In this report, we identify key constructs relevant to ensuring environmental fitness. After describing types of environmental stressors and potential workplace injuries, we address research on preventive and protective factors. Finally, we review documented interventions that could promote environmental fitness.

The results of these reports should be relevant to Air Force leaders who are tasked with monitoring and supporting the well-being of active duty, reserve and guard Airmen, and Air Force civilian employees, as well as their families. The results of our studies may also help broaden the scope of research on resilience and help Airmen and their families achieve optimal environmental fitness. The research described in this report was conducted within the Manpower, Personnel, and Training Program of RAND Project AIR FORCE as part of a fiscal year 2011 study titled "Program and Facility Support for Air Force Personnel and Family Resiliency."

RAND Project AIR FORCE

RAND Project AIR FORCE (PAF), a division of the RAND Corporation, is the U.S. Air Force's federally funded research and development center for studies and analyses. PAF provides the Air Force with independent analyses of policy alternatives affecting the development, employment, combat readiness, and support of current and future air, space, and cyber forces. Research is conducted in four programs: Force Modernization and Employment; Manpower, Personnel, and Training; Resource Management; and Strategy and Doctrine. The research reported here was prepared under contract FA7014-06-C-0001.

Additional information about PAF is available on our website: http://www.rand.org/paf/

Table of Contents

Summary

Environmental fitness, as it applies to Airmen, their families, and Air Force civilians, can be defined as the knowledge, skills, and behaviors needed to successfully protect against stress associated with one's environment or to successfully withstand the stressors that are encountered. Environmental stressors of particular concern to the Air Force may include those resulting from temperature, noise, altitude, chemicals, and the workplace. For some of these, exposure metrics are readily available. For others, such as chemical exposure, measurements are more difficult to make and may require extensive data or invasive methods (e.g., blood work) to assess exposure. As a result, the Air Force must carefully consider which metrics are most appropriate, and most economical, to use.

Key resilience factors for environmental fitness can be grouped into two categories: (1) prevention of exposure to environmental stressors and hazards and (2) protection against environmental stressors and hazards. Prevention typically addresses actions that can mitigate environmental stress before personnel encounter it, whereas protection mitigates environmental stress when personnel encounter it.

The prevention measures we consider relate to safety culture and climate, safety training and education, financial incentives to prevent injury, and compliance with safety standards and regulations. Management commitment to safety is key to positive outcomes. Safety training and education can have an effect if that training is targeted to specific behaviors (e.g., using safety goggles). No evidence suggests that financial incentives increase safety or reduce accidents or injuries. Safety inspections with corporate penalties reduce workplace injuries in the short term, especially if they are associated with use of personal protective equipment (PPE), but compliance with safety standards is not always linked to a reduction in workplace injury. The Air Force can capitalize on this research by ensuring that Airmen are properly educated on using safety equipment when necessary and that safety inspections are conducted regularly.

The protection measures we consider include use of PPE, acclimatization and tolerance, and ergonomics. The effectiveness of PPE depends largely on whether it is used properly and if it is job- or industry-specific. Acclimatization and tolerance can reduce the negative effect of certain environmental stressors, such as temperature and altitude. Workplace ergonomics is associated with preventing musculoskeletal problems and reducing injuries.

Appropriate use of PPE is the most directly relevant environmental fitness factor in preventing workplace injury. A number of determinants influence compliance with PPE standards, including individual characteristics (e.g., sociodemographics, attitudes and beliefs, knowledge, and education), job characteristics (e.g., experience level, skill, cognitive demands, workload, work stress), and organizational characteristics (e.g., training, peer review, management support, safety and culture climate). The military can influence each of these.

Individuals in the military undergo an indoctrination period, during which they may be taught proper safety compliance and culture, which the military may also continue to emphasize over time.

In improving the resilience of Airmen to environmental stressors, the Air Force should first decide which stressors it wishes to address, including where to prioritize data-collection efforts about effects. Second, the Air Force should focus on predictors of PPE use that cut across all types of equipment and jobs and design interventions accordingly. Third, the Air Force can target some strategies to the most relevant subgroups. All such strategies should help build a connection between a safety climate, where individuals accept the importance of safety, and a safety culture, where the institution is committed to safety.

Acknowledgments

This research was sponsored by the Air Force Resilience office and was led by Mr. Brian P. Borda for a significant portion of the study period and by Air Force Surgeon General Lt Gen (Dr.) Charles B. Green, and Mr. William H. Booth, the Deputy Assistant Secretary of the Air Force for Force Management Integration (SAF/MRM).

We would like to thank the action officers from the sponsoring offices for their role in shaping the research agenda and providing feedback on interim and final briefings of the research findings. Those officers are Maj Kirby Bowling, our primary contact from the Air Force Resilience office; Col John Forbes and Lt Col David Dickey from the Air Force Surgeon General's office; and Linda Stephens-Jones from SAF/MRM. We also appreciate the insights and recommendations from Ms. Eliza Nesmith while she was in the Air Force Services, and Lt Col Shawn Campbell while he served in the SAF/MRM office.

RAND's Sarah Meadows and Laura Miller led the overall research effort on resilience and provided extensive feedback on a previous draft of this manuscript. Ramya Chari provided helpful comments on an earlier draft. Donna White and Hosay Salam Yaqub provided valuable assistance formatting the manuscript and the bibliography for publication.

We would also like to thank our reviewers, Dr. Al Ozonoff, Dr. Joshua E.J. Buckman, and Ms. Rachel Burns for their astute reviews and helpful feedback on the report, which greatly strengthened the quality of this document.

Abbreviations

BLS	Bureau of Labor Statistics
DART	days away/restricted or transfer
DAW	days away from work
db	Decibel
DCoE	Defense Centers of Excellence for Psychological Health and Traumatic Brain Injury
DoD	Department of Defense
FTE	full-time employee
GAO	Government Accountability Office
HPD	hearing-protection device
IWH	Institute for Work and Health
JP	jet propellant
mg/m^3	milligrams per cubic meter
MRL	minimal risk level
NIOSH	National Institute for Occupational Safety and Health
OSHA	Occupational Safety and Health Administration
PE	participatory ergonomics
PPE	personal protective equipment
PSI	Physiological Strain Index
SOII	Survey of Occupational Injuries and Illnesses
TFF	Total Force Fitness

1. The Context of This Report[1]

This report is one of a series designed to support Air Force leaders in promoting resilience among Airmen, its civilian employees, and Air Force family members. The research sponsors requested that RAND assess the current resilience-related constructs and measures in the scientific literature and report any evidence of initiatives that promote resilience across a number of domains. We did not limit our search to research conducted in military settings or with military personnel, as Air Force leaders sought the potential opportunity to apply results of these studies to a population that had not yet been addressed (i.e., Airmen). Further, many Air Force services support Air Force civilians and family members, and thus the results of civilian studies would apply to these populations.

This study adopts the Air Force definition of resilience: "the ability to withstand, recover and/or grow in the face of stressors and changing demands."[2] By focusing on resilience, the armed forces aim to expand their care to ensure the well-being of military personnel and their families through preventive measures and not just by treating members after they begin to experience negative outcomes (e.g., depression, anxiety, insomnia, substance abuse, post-traumatic stress disorder, or suicidal ideation).

Admiral Michael Mullen, Chairman of the Joint Chiefs of Staff from 2007 to 2011, outlined the concept of Total Force Fitness (TFF) in a special issue of the journal *Military Medicine*: "A total force that has achieved total fitness is healthy, ready, and resilient; capable of meeting challenges and surviving threats" (Mullen, 2010, p. 1). This notion of "fitness" is directly related to the concept of resilience. The same issue of *Military Medicine* also reflected the collective effort of scholars, health professionals, and military personnel, who outlined eight domains of TFF: medical, nutritional, environmental, physical, social, spiritual, behavioral, and psychological. This framework expands on the traditional conceptualization of resilience by looking beyond the psychological realm to also emphasize the mind-body connection and the interdependence of each of the eight domains.

The research sponsors requested that RAND adopt these eight fitness domains as the organizing framework for our literature review. We followed this general framework, although in some cases we adapted the scope of a domain to better reflect the relevant

---

[1] Adapted from Meadows, Miller, and Robson (2015).

[2] The Air Force adopted this definition, which was developed by the Defense Centers of Excellence for Psychological Health and Traumatic Brain Injury (DCoE, 2011).

research. Thus, this study resulted in eight reports, each focusing on resilience-related research in one of the TFF domains, but we note that not all of these domains are mutually exclusive. These eight reports define each domain and address the following interrelated topics:

- medical: preventive care, the presence and management of injuries, chronic conditions, and barriers and bridges to accessing appropriate quality health care (Shih, Meadows, and Martin, 2013)
- nutritional: food intake, dietary patterns and behavior, the food environment (Flórez, Shih, and Martin, 2014)
- environmental: environmental stressors and potential workplace injuries and preventive and protective factors (Shih et al., 2015)
- physical: physical activity and fitness (Robson, 2013)
- social: social fitness and social support from family, friends, coworkers/unit members, neighbors, and cybercommunities (McGene, 2013)
- spiritual: spiritual worldview, personal religious or spiritual practices and rituals, support from a spiritual community, and spiritual coping (Yeung and Martin, 2013)
- behavioral: health behaviors related to sleep and to drug, alcohol, and tobacco use (Robson and Salcedo, 2014)
- psychological: self-regulation, positive and negative affect, perceived control, self-efficacy, self-esteem, optimism, adaptability, self-awareness, and emotional intelligence (Robson, 2014)

These reports are not intended to be comprehensive reviews of the entire literature within a domain. Rather, they focus on those studies that consider the stress-buffering aspects of each domain, regardless of whether the term *resilience* is specifically used. This expanded the scope of the reviews to include a broader range of studies and also allowed for differences in the terminology used across different disciplines (e.g., stress management, hardiness). We sought evidence both on the main effects of resilience factors in each domain (i.e., those that promote general well-being) and on the indirect or interactive effects (i.e., those that buffer the negative effects of stress).

Because the Air Force commissioned this research to specifically address individuals' capacity to be resilient, and thus their well-being, our reports do not address whether or how fitness in each of the eight TFF domains could be linked to other outcomes of interest to the military, such as performance, discipline, unit readiness, personnel costs, attrition, or retention. Those worthy topics were beyond the scope of this project.

Some other important parameters shaped this literature review. First, across the study, we focused on research from the past decade, although older studies are included, particularly landmark studies that still define the research landscape or where a particular line of inquiry has been dormant in recent years. Second, we prioritized research on adults in the United States. Research on children was included where particularly germane (e.g., in discussions of family as a form of social support), and, occasionally, research on adults in other Western nations is referenced or subsumed within a large study. Research on elderly populations was generally excluded. Third, we prioritized literature reviews, meta-analyses, and on-going bodies of research over more singular smaller-scale studies.

The search for evidence on ways to promote resilience in each domain included both actions that individuals could take as well as actions that organizations could take, such as information campaigns, policies, directives, programs, initiatives, facilities, or other resources. We did not filter out evidence related to Air Force practices already under way, as the Air Force was interested both in research related to existing practices and in research that might suggest new paths for promoting resilience. Our aim was not to collect examples of creative or promising initiatives at large but to seek scholarly publications assessing the stress-buffering capacity of initiatives. Thus, in general, this collection of reviews does not address initiatives that have not yet been evaluated for their effect.

Building on the foundation of the eight reports that assess the scientific literature in each domain, RAND prepared an overarching report that brings together the highlights of these reviews and examines their relevance to current Air Force metrics and programs. That ninth report, *Airman and Family Resilience: Lessons from the Scientific Literature* (Meadows, Miller, and Robson, 2015), provides a more in-depth introduction to resilience concepts and research, presents our model of the relationship between resilience and TFF, documents established and emerging Air Force resiliency efforts, and reviews Air Force metrics for tracking the resiliency of Air Force personnel and their families. By comparing the information we found in the research literature to Air Force practices, we were able to provide recommendations to support the development of initiatives to promote resilience across the Air Force. Although the overview report contains Air Force–specific recommendations that take into account all eight domains and existing Air Force practices, some are applicable to the military more generally and are highlighted at the end of this report.

Our review of environmental-fitness metrics and interventions began by identifying several key questions, such as "What environmental stressors contribute to poor well-being in service members?" and "What kinds of measures can mitigate environmental stressors?" These questions resulted in several groups of search terms: (1) stress, resilience, well-being (stress buffer, resilience, fitness, readiness, coping), (2) environmental stressors (chemicals, injury, occupational health, workplace environments, acclimatization), (3) programs (Air Force Instruction, Department of Defense [DoD] Directive, evidence-based programs, prevention, interventions, policies, campaign, disease management, screening. health education), and (4) terms related to the specific populations of interest (DoD, military, Air Force, service members, Airmen, children). We entered combinations of these terms into search engines such as PubMed, Web of Science, and Google Scholar.

In our search, we prioritized review studies and then empirical studies. To ensure that we captured as many existing studies as possible, we conducted an iterative search by examining the reference lists of all retrieved articles. We searched for working papers and reports published by governmental and nongovernmental organizations, in addition to peer-reviewed publications.

Using this approach, we organize the remainder of this report around two constructs of environmental fitness: *prevention* of exposure to environmental stressors or hazards (e.g., safety culture and climate, safety training and education, financial incentives, safety standards), and *protection* against environmental stressors and hazards already present in an environment (e.g., use of personal protective equipment [PPE], acclimatization and tolerance, ergonomics). We focus on these two constructs because they capture the ability to function in an environment where exposure to potentially deleterious stress is likely to occur. Although we include education related to PPE and its use, we do not discuss different brands or models of particular types of PPE (e.g., exposure-specific devices, such as N95 respirators) because these have specific regulations to determine their effectiveness.

Neither do we include research on the results of inadequate prevention or protection or how well one's body may process exposures. Therefore, we do not include biological markers that may indicate exposure to environmental toxins (e.g., lead or mercury) because these are not measures of fitness or resilience. The accompanying reports on medical fitness (Shih, Meadows, and Martin, 2013) and nutritional fitness (Flórez, Shih, and Martin, 2014) discuss biological stressors within the medical and nutritional domains.

Existing research on resilience factors in the environmental domain is much less well established and conclusive than that for many other fitness domains. Currently, no definitive metrics of environmental fitness exist for service members (O'Conner et al., 2010; May et al., 2004), and few metrics exist to measure fitness for work among civilians (Serra et al., 2007).[3] As a result, this report is more speculative than others in the series of reports on TFF metrics.

---

[3] Serra et al. (2007, p. 304) define fitness for work as "the determination of whether an individual is fit to perform his or her tasks without risk to self or others."

In the next chapter, we preview the contents of this report and briefly discuss examples of environmental stressors that deployed Airmen, nondeployed Airmen, their families, and Air Force civilians may face. In the third and fourth chapters of the report, we discuss factors that are generally linked to environmental fitness and, when necessary, can be used to mitigate the consequences of exposure to environmental stressors. These chapters also provide examples of metrics to assess the environmental-fitness factors we discuss. Finally, we review interventions that have been shown to improve environmental fitness, focusing primarily on the appropriate use of PPE.

2. Environmental Stressors

"The truly healthy environment is not merely safe but stimulating."
— William H. Stewart, Physician

Environmental fitness can be defined as, "the ability to perform mission-specific duties in any environment and withstand the multiple stressors of deployment and war" (O'Conner et al., 2010, p. 57). Although this definition specifically emphasizes deployed Airmen and in-theater operations, environmental fitness is also applicable to Airmen who are not deployed, to Air Force spouses and other family members,[4] and to civilians employed by the Air Force. We therefore define environmental fitness to include the knowledge, skills, and behaviors necessary to successfully protect against stress associated with one's environment. In some contexts, organizational practices are also directly relevant to an individual's ability to handle environmental stressors and ultimately promote environmental fitness.

In noting examples of environmental stressors, we focus on those that are most relevant to Airmen. Other types of stressors are not covered here (e.g., those related to the deployment experience). For example, the cognitive and emotional repercussions of deployment stress would fall into the psychological domain (Robson, 2014).

Among Airmen, especially those who are deployed, environmental stressors can be classified as physical (e.g., temperature, noise, altitude), biological (e.g., food, water, vector-borne disease), or chemical (e.g., occupational and environmental contaminants) (see Lounsbury, 2003). Many, but not all, of these stressors can be anticipated, either before deployment or on entry into the workplace. For those that cannot, Airmen must be prepared, or environmentally fit. Biological stressors are covered in more depth in companion reports in this series on nutritional (Flórez, Shih, and Martin, 2014) and medical fitness (Shih, Meadows, and Martin, 2013). We therefore focus here on chemical and physical stressors.

---

[4] Because most stressors in the environmental domain pertain to job- or occupational-related situations, the domain is less relevant to children and youths than are other domains (e.g., psychological, social). Yet children may spend much of their time at school or at child-care facilities and thus be exposed to environmental stress factors in these locations. Children and older youths may also be exposed to physical conditions associated with their environments, such as extreme heat or cold, and thus some of the research that we review may be relevant to them. However, in general we limit our discussion of the environmental domain to adults in work-related environments.

We consider five types of physical environmental stressors faced by military personnel: temperature (heat or cold), noise, altitude, chemicals, and workplace environments in which injuries or death may occur.

Temperature

Of all heat-related illnesses, heat stroke is by far the most serious. Heat stroke occurs when the body is unable to regulate temperature and the cardiovascular system is overstressed by the competing needs of thermoregulation and metabolic requirements, in some cases leading to death (Smith, Manning, and Petruzzello, 2001). In 2005, the U.S. Army reported more than 1,100 cases of heat injury, including 204 cases of heat stroke (U.S. Army, 2006).

The physiological causes of heat stroke and other heat-related illnesses are well known. Environmentally, these disorders are associated with prolonged exposure to extreme heat or extreme heat and high humidity, which does not allow the body to cool itself normally. Heat stress can also result from improper use of PPE (Muza, Banderet, and Cadarette, 2001; Givoni and Goldman, 1972) or lack of heat acclimatization. Individuals who are not heat acclimated tend to have poor skin blood flow and lower sweat rates, which lead to increased core body temperatures and heart rate in response to heat stress (Frisancho, 1993).

Other common sequela of heat-related problems include dehydration, sleep disturbance, and chronic suffering from more common although less severe symptoms, such as nausea, vomiting, hyperirritability, dizziness, and dermatological abrasions. These affect not only physical health but also psychological health and job performance. The reduction in alertness, concentration, reaction time, and judgment means that when experiencing adverse reactions to heat, personnel will be more at risk when operating dangerous machinery or weapons and when driving.

In addition to heat injuries, Airmen involved in operations in desert or mountainous regions may also experience cold-related injuries, as some locations have large temperature ranges and fluctuations between daytime and nighttime. This creates a more complicated environment for the health and performance of Air Force members.

Noise

Chronic exposure to noise at levels above 85 decibels (db) can cause permanent hearing loss. Higher exposure levels of even a few hours per day cause hearing damage. An additional auditory issue for deployed service members is the risk of tympanic membrane perforation resulting from improvised-explosive-device blast overpressure (Ritenour et al., 2008).

The U.S. Government Accountability Office (GAO, 2011) reported that hearing impairments were one of the most common reasons for Veteran's Health Administration disability benefits, with payments exceeding $1.1 billion per year. In 2009, there were more than 50,000 awards for hearing loss and more than 70,000 for tinnitus (ringing in the ear).

Hearing is essential for many military tasks, including the differentiation of friendly from enemy fire and acting as a warning sense. The negative effects of hearing loss include greater susceptibility to paranoia and psychotic-spectrum disorders (Zimbardo, Andersen, and Kabat, 1981; Freeman et al., 2008). The effects of tinnitus vary from mild to severe and can be permanent. In some cases, hearing loss can be ameliorated with a hearing aid. A 2002 Institute of Medicine study found that even among service members enrolled in hearing conservation programs, 10 to 18 percent still experienced a significant shift in their hearing threshold (Humes, Joellenbeck, and Durch, 2005). This range was two to five times as large as rates considered to be appropriate in industrial hearing conservation programs.

Noise is also a common problem for nondeployed Airmen and civilians who work in certain industrial occupations (Middendorf, 2004). A recent study using data from the National Health and Nutrition Examination Survey reported that 22 million, or 17 percent, of workers reported exposure to hazardous noise, defined as having to speak in a raised voice to be heard (Tak, Davis, and Calvert, 2009). One-third of the workers in the study said that they did not use hearing-protection devices (HPDs). In Great Britain, one study of 22,000 people 5–64 years of age found that 8 percent had hearing problems (Palmer et al., 2002), with the prevalence of such problems increasing with the number of years spent in noisy jobs. In addition to potentially causing hearing loss, high levels of workplace noise appear to cause more accidents and have been linked to increases in blood pressure (Suter, 2008).

Altitude

Perhaps a unique physical environmental stressor among Airmen is that of altitude. As altitude increases, oxygen pressure decreases, making less oxygen available to the body. Above 8,000 feet, this pressure change can have serious physical and cognitive consequences for the human body (i.e., hypobaric hypoxia). Altitude-related illnesses include acute mountain sickness, high-altitude pulmonary edema, and high-altitude cerebral edema. Although acclimatization can counteract some effects of hypoxia, the biological and genetic components of serious altitude sickness are still not well understood (Friedl and Penetar, 2008). Although pilots use oxygen systems at high altitude, the effects of altitude-related illness also apply to Airmen on bases at high altitudes or those in noncombat, support, or service-support roles working on the ground at high altitudes. These Airmen are also vulnerable to hypoxic conditions (Rock, 2002) and may not be as aware as pilots of the signs and symptoms.

Chemicals

Another physical environmental stressor more prevalent in the Air Force than elsewhere is jet-propellant (JP) fuel, a complex mixture of numerous hydrocarbon compounds and additives (Proctor et al., 2011; Maule et al., 2013). Some studies suggest that JP-8, the primary jet fuel used by the U.S. military, is potentially toxic to the immune, respiratory, and nervous systems (Merchant-Borna et al., 2011). To date, numerous protective and preventive strategies (e.g., federal exposure limits; workplace-procedure protocols; protective gear such as goggles, respirator use, gloves, and coveralls) have been put in place to minimize acutely toxic exposure levels by the Occupational Safety and Health Administration (OSHA) and the Air Force Office of Safety and Health. Specifically, these agencies regulate levels of all petroleum products including JP-8 in private-sector workplaces and in Air Force workplaces, respectively. The maximum allowable amount of petroleum products in workroom air during an 8-hour workday, 40-hour workweek, is 400 milligrams per cubic meter (mg/m^3). The Agency for Toxic Substances and Disease Registry (2008) has derived an intermediate-duration inhalation minimal risk level (MRL) of 3 mg/m^3 for JP-8. An MRL is an estimate of daily human exposure to a substance over a specific period that is likely to be without an appreciable risk of adverse effects (e.g., noncarcinogenic).

Several techniques can determine JP-8 exposure levels. These include measuring exposure through breathing zone samples (Smith et al., 2010), skin samples (Chao et al., 2006; Chao, Gibson, and Nylander-French, 2005), exhaled breath (Pleil, Smith, and Zelnick, 2000; Tu et al., 2004), and urinary biomarkers (Serdar et al., 2003; Smith et al., 2012). However, most of these tests are not widely available and are used primarily for research

Urinary biomarkers, in particular, may provide a surrogate measure for combined dermal and inhalation JP-8 exposure. One study found that urinary 1- and 2-naphthol levels accurately reflect JP-8 exposure during the work-shift and may be useful surrogates of JP-8 exposure (Smith et al., 2012). Another study that compared three biomarkers of JP-8 exposure found 2-methoxyethoxy acetic acid to be a more accurate or appropriate urinary biomarker than S-benzylmercapturic acid and S-phenylmercapturic acid for measuring JP-8 exposure (B'Hymer et al., 2012).

Measurement of chemical exposures can be done with exposure modeling and biomarkers of exposure. Both are proxies for actual, personal exposures. Biomarkers are imperfect because of differences in the way individuals metabolize chemicals or because of their personal toxicodynamics. Biomarkers reflect how the body processes, absorbs, or excretes chemicals after exposures.

To determine individual levels of resilience to exposures, one would need to know levels of exposure, body burden, and toxicodynamics. Some individuals may absorb chemicals more quickly, process them more efficiently, or excrete them more effectively. Others may be more vulnerable to negative health effects because of pre-existing health conditions.

Hazardous Workplace Environments

Deployed Airmen are not the only individuals who may encounter environmental stressors. Civilians, especially those with certain occupations (e.g., stock and material handlers, nursing aides and orderlies, truck drivers, police officers, construction laborers), and those who work outdoors are also exposed to potentially hazardous environmental conditions in the course of their jobs. One of the few ways to measure exposure to environmental stressors associated with employment is to focus on occupational injuries and deaths.

Workplace injuries are not themselves environmental stressors but are often thought to be the result of such stressors. Workplace-injury prevalence rates may indicate environmental fitness at a group (e.g., unit) level. In lieu of primary data analyses of restricted datasets such as those comprised in the *Total Army Injury and Health Outcomes Database*, we reviewed publically available data on injuries. The Census of Fatal Occupational Injuries by the U.S. Bureau of Labor Statistics (BLS, 2012) reports that fatal occupational injuries for resident armed forces in 2012 were mostly attributable to transportation incidents.

One major measure of the incidence of nonfatal occupational injuries in the United States is the annual Survey of Occupational Injuries and Illnesses (SOII), also conducted by the BLS. OSHA requires that employers record three types of injuries: (1) all injuries that involve days away from work (DAW cases), (2) cases with restricted work activity or job transfer (DART[5]), and (3) cases with only medical treatment (beyond first aid). The BLS collects these injury and illness records from a sample of establishments (about 200,000 in recent years) to calculate national rates and state rates (for all but eight states)

---

[5] The DART describes the number of recordable injuries and illnesses per 100 full-time employees (FTEs) that resulted in days away from work, restricted activity at work, or a job transfer during a given period of time.

by major industry categories. For DAW injuries, the BLS also publishes data about injury causes and nature, part of body affected, and the type of equipment involved, along with some demographic information about those injured and the median number of days lost for different categories. Table 2.1 shows the number and rate of nonfatal occupational injuries reported to BLS through the OSHA system for the seven occupational groups with the most DAW injuries.

Table 2.1. Occupations with the Most DAW Cases and Leading Event or Exposure

Occupation	Number of Cases	Incidence per 1,000 FTE	Leading Event (% of Total)
Laborers and freight, stock, and material movers	64,910	4.1	Contact with equipment (32%) Overexertion (32%)
Nursing aides, orderlies, and attendants	50,620	4.6	Overexertion (48%) Fall on same level (17%)
Janitors and cleaners (except maids and housekeeping)	48,180	3.2	Overexertion (29%) Contact with object/equipment (21%)
Truck drivers: heavy and tractor-trailer	47,790	3.3	Overexertion (23%) Contact with object/equipment (20%)
Police and sheriff's patrol officers	35,590	6.0	Assaults/violent acts (23%) Transportation incidents (18%)
Truck drivers: light or delivery services	32,210	4.1	Overexertion (28%) Contact with object/equipment (16%)
Construction laborers	26,690	3.8	Contact with object/equipment (43%) Overexertion (17%)

SOURCE$$$ OS$E009).$$

The occupations listed in Table 2.1 experienced 25 percent of all DAW cases in the United States (excluding federal-government employment). Their rates far exceeded the national DAW rate of 1.2 per 100 FTEs. The most common cause of DAW injuries is "overexertion," accounting for 23 percent of the total. This category includes injuries resulting from lifting, bending, stretching, pushing, and pulling. These injuries, along with those caused by repetitive motion, are musculoskeletal injuries that might be addressed by ergonomic measures. However, OSHA does not have any standards that address these hazards, and its effort to promulgate an ergonomics standard was overturned in early 2001.

Some researchers claim that the SOII substantially undercounts injuries, perhaps by as much as 50 percent (Boden and Ozonoff, 2008), but analysts at the BLS claim that the problem is much smaller (Boden, Nestoriak, and Pierce, 2010). Certain biases in the reporting are clear, however. First, smaller establishments are more likely than larger establishments to underreport (Mendeloff et al., 2006). Second, states in the South and Appalachia underreport accidents more than other states, whereas states in the Northwest underreport less (Mendeloff and Burns, 2012).

There is no way to establish the "true" number of nonfatal injuries. The number of reported injuries is affected by cultural, economic, and social questions (Azanoff, Levenstein, and Wegman, 2002). For example: Are injuries viewed as work-related? Do workers face sanctions for reporting injuries? What is the cost-benefit calculus for taking time off work? Reported lost workday injuries are about 15 percent higher in states that compensate workers after three days off work than in states that compensate only after seven days or more (LaTourette and Mendeloff, 2008).

The Census of Fatal Occupational Injuries, also conducted by BLS, reports on the causes of occupational deaths. In 2012, transportation incidents accounted for 39 percent of fatal occupational injuries, and violence accounted for 17 percent (BLS, 2012). Most violence-related deaths were homicides committed during robberies, although shootings by disgruntled employees typically receive the most media coverage.

The more traditional occupational causes of death span a wide spectrum. Falls, especially in construction, are the most distinct category, but electrocutions, fires and explosions, and toxic exposures are also reported. Many other deaths occur as a result of diseases with occupational causes. Almost all of these are diseases with long development or latency periods, so current diseases usually reflect past exposures more than current ones. Estimates of the number of such diseases vary widely. With a few major exceptions (e.g., asbestosis, mesothelioma), diseases are not uniquely occupational in origin. Thus, estimates must be made through epidemiological studies of the risks faced by exposed workers relative to those unexposed. Several studies have suggested that the proportion of cancer deaths resulting from occupational exposures ranges from 2 to 5 percent (Rushton et al., 2010; Doll and Peto, 1981). Estimates on heart-disease deaths caused by work are even more speculative (Suter, 2008).

BLS also collects information on exposure to harmful substances or environments that are associated with loss-of-time injuries. Most of the top 15 causes for loss-of-time injuries on private-sector jobs in 2009 (excluding agriculture) resulted from failure to wear protective equipment. These causes included contact with hot objects, exposure to radiation (e.g., ultraviolet radiation absorbed in the cornea of an eye through welding), inhalation of toxic substances, contact with electricity, contact with heat, exposure to noise (single incident), and contact with cold or cold objects (BLS, 2009). These data suggest that proper use of PPE could reduce workplace injuries.

Summary

Our work focused on key environmental stressors—including temperature (heat or cold), noise, altitude, chemicals, and workplace environments—in which injuries or deaths may occur. It was outside the scope of this report to review all possible environmental stressors that Airmen may experience. Of course, there are other stressors related to the general environment of serving in the military (e.g., being deployed, working long hours, separation from family and other forms of social support) and many of these other stressors are addressed in other reports in this series.

Our review of the literature found that, for some specific types of environmental stressors, exposure metrics (e.g., heat stroke, hearing gloss, injuries per FTE) are readily available. However, others, such as chemical exposure, are more difficult and require far more data and invasive methods (e.g., blood work) to assess exposure.

The Air Force must carefully consider which metrics are most appropriate, and most economical, to collect and use. Unfortunately, these measures can only indicate whether an Airmen has already been exposed to a potentially negative stimulus, situation, or stress. We next discuss what the Air Force and Airmen might do to prevent negative exposures and maximize environmental fitness (i.e., resilience resources in the environmental-fitness domain).

3. Key Resilience Factors: Prevention

Several individual and organizational factors can both prevent and protect individuals from environmental stressors. Preventive measures are those that reduce the risk of experiencing an environmental stressor before it is encountered. A protective measure is one that, when a stressor is present, can counteract its negative effects. The distinction is important because not all environmental stressors can be prevented, even if precautionary measures are taken. In this chapter, we focus on preventive measures, including safety culture and climate, safety training and education, financial incentives to prevent injuries, and compliance with safety regulations. The following chapter focuses on protective measures.

Safety Culture and Climate

The concept of safety culture has been developed to describe an organizational commitment to safe practices for preventing injuries and exposures to potentially dangerous workplace situations (e.g., chemical exposures). Safety culture generally focuses on overt and tangible management commitment to safety, its transmission to line supervisors, and the involvement of employees.

Pidgeon (1997) defines safety culture as organizational features that seek to prevent "complex" accidents, e.g., those requiring external investigation rather than internal handling. Others view the term as more widely applicable to all types of safety performance. Safety culture became a more prominent issue after the Baker Commission's highly critical 2007 report on British Petroleum after an explosion at its Texas City, Texas, refinery.

Safety climate is defined more narrowly than safety culture and from the perspective of the employee. Safety climate includes employee perceptions of organizational safety policies and practices (Zohar, 1980, 2010). The military has the unenviable position of teaching its members to overcome fear and engage in risky situations (e.g., combat), often without regard to personal safety, while promoting safe work environments and reducing risk.

One important impetus for a safety climate has been the search for "leading indicators" for safety and health (i.e., indicators that can be quickly monitored, assessed, and used as feedback in decisionmaking). These are posed in contrast to the traditional measures of safety and health performance (e.g., deaths, injuries, and illnesses that have occurred in the past), which typically have a very long lag time between the safety event and calculation of the indicator.

Leading indicators of safety climate could provide very valuable guidance for improving environmental safety policies and practices. Leading indicators can also provide more timely feedback on a firm's safety program and its direction. Safety-climate metrics could become a surrogate for those based on injury outcomes, which are not known immediately and are subject to random variation, making it difficult to learn whether safety is improving and which policies, practices, or initiatives contributed to its improvement.

The most recent and careful meta-analysis of safety climate studies has helped to clarify the research in several ways. Beus et al. (2010) examined three categories of studies. The first used injuries to predict individual ratings of safety climate, management commitment to safety, management safety practices, coworker safety, safety communication, safety training, and housekeeping. The second used injuries to predict organization-level safety climate and suggested that general safety policy and safety procedures are promising measures that contribute to safety climate. The third used organizational-safety climate, particularly management commitment to safety and safety reporting, to predict injuries. Some studies within each of these three categories examined the role of effect modification variables, or variables that could exacerbate or buffer relationships between injuries and the individual safety climate. These studies suggest that metrics of safety climate should incorporate measures of management commitment, one of the most robust effect modifiers (also referred to as moderators).

Beus et al. (2010) also found that the predictive value of the organizational-safety climate for injury rates declined sharply as the length of time used to calculate injury rates increased. In other words, organizational-safety-climate measures of data are better at predicting the injury rate when they are based on the preceding 12 months than when they are based on the preceding 24 months. This finding is consistent with the notion that the safety-climate measure is a "snapshot."

It is often useful to get judgments on the quality of a safety effort in a simple fashion. The Institute for Work and Health (IWH, 2011, p. 5) has designed a tool for collecting information on a firm's commitment to safety that one company informant can complete. Its eight items ask informants whether the following statements are true:

1. Formal safety audits at regular intervals are part of our business.
2. Everyone at the organization values ongoing safety improvement in this organization.
3. The organization considers safety at least as important as production and quality in the way work is done.
4. Workers and supervisors have the information they need to work safely.

5. Employees are always involved in decisions affecting their health and safety.
6. Those in charge of safety have the authority to make the changes they have identified as necessary.
7. Those who act safely receive positive recognition.
8. Everyone has the tools and/or equipment they need to complete their work safely.

This study's examination of the validity of the questionnaire, across roughly 650 firms whose injury rates were tracked over four years, found that firms with summary scores in the highest quartile, had, on average, a 25 percent lower injury rate than the firms in the bottom quartile. A promising feature of the questionnaire was that summary scores were similar across industries and across size categories of firms, suggesting that it has high construct validity. However, injury data here preceded the judgments about the firm, and thus the issue of whether injuries are indeed "leading" indicators of safety is moot.

There is no consensus on how to conduct safety-climate surveys, other than that employees should complete them and describe their views of how well the firm carries out various safety functions and how strong its commitment to safety is. Some surveys are a census of all employees but others use random samples. Some surveys generate a single measure for the whole establishment, or even for the whole firm, whereas others develop measures for work groups. The number of questions can vary from 10 to more than 50. Some firms conduct safety surveys annually; others conduct cross-sectional, one-time surveys. The National Safety Council, which has conducted hundreds of safety-climate studies, uses an instrument with 50 items covering such topics as senior management leadership and commitment, supervisory participation, employee involvement, safety programs and activities, and safety and organizational climate (National Safety Council, 2011).

Although there is little consensus on how to measure the safety climate, the involvement of managers or leaders in the military to establish it remains important. If Air Force leaders are not directly involved in enforcing measures to protect safety, the rest of the organization will not follow.

Safety Training and Education

One of the clearest findings in the safety literature is that inexperienced workers are at greater risk of injury (Breslin and Smith, 2007). This suggests that employers should place a high premium on safety training for new hires or for employees taking on new jobs. For the Air Force, this means that junior enlisted personnel may be more vulnerable to injury and that the greatest emphasis on safety and supervision should be placed on those at the lowest skill levels.

Unfortunately, the literature on safety training provides little guidance on program quality. A systematic review by IWH and the National Institute for Occupational Safety and Health (NIOSH) found a lack of high-quality, randomized-control trials on safety training and effectiveness (Robson et al., 2010). The report focused on 14 studies of varying populations, interventions, and outcomes, making it difficult to reach clear, generalizable conclusions. For three of the four outcomes examined—knowledge, attitudes, and health—the strength of evidence to assess the effects of training was judged "insufficient," meaning that the methodological quality of the reviewed studies was low, there were few studies to review, and reported effects were inconsistent (i.e., both positive and negative). Thus, the review found that occupational health and safety training on its own did not have a direct effect on health by reducing the number of injuries or symptoms. Nevertheless, the review found that training had a "strong" positive effect on targeted behavior, suggesting that there is an indirect link between it and health. The review found insufficient evidence to determine whether level of engagement or intensity of training (i.e., single versus multiple training sessions) was more effective.

Financial Incentives for Injury Prevention

Some organizations use financial incentives to increase workplace health and safety and to reduce injures. Financial incentives for employees can include rewards for groups of workers who have no reported injuries for a specific period of time. Supervisor and manager salaries or bonuses may be directly pegged to the safety outcomes reported for the units they oversee. Firms as a whole may also benefit financially from savings in workers' compensation premiums and in reductions in other related costs of injuries.

At the same time, financial incentives could unintentionally encourage employees to underreport injuries to capitalize on the incentive program. Many Air Force installations have a "mishap-free" day tally, but not many have an incentive program. Although the military is prevented from offering monetary rewards for safety, it can use other incentives, such as a pass or liberty (day off) or recognition through awards. Partnering with outdoor recreation or other base services may also provide incentives for safety.

The Air Force currently employs OSHA's Voluntary Protection Program, an award program for exemplary safety and health management systems (see, for example, Wright-Patterson Air Force Base, undated). The Federal Aviation Administration uses voluntary reporting programs such as the National Aeronautics and Space Administration's Aviation Safety Reporting System and a Voluntary Self-Disclosure in which mistakes or violations can be reported with immunity from civil penalties. The use of these nonpunitive programs has been cited as improving air safety (U.S. House Committee on Transportation and Infrastructure, 2007).

Studies that have evaluated the value of nonvoluntary or incentive programs have shown mixed results. A 1998 study commissioned by OSHA examined nine incentive programs with awards based on injury outcomes and 16 with awards based on observance of safety procedures and injury outcomes; it found no good evidence that the programs had any effect (OSHA, 1999). However, a study of the U.S. construction industry suggests that safety-incentive programs, particularly those with tangible awards (e.g., cash, gifts, prizes), improved several safety-performance metrics including fewer lost workdays and recordable incidence rates, and declines in these incidence rates were greater over a two-year period. When only tangible awards (cash, lottery, gifts, prizes) were offered, safety performance was better and incidence rates were lower than when both tangible and intangible items (trophies, certificates, time off, parties) were offered. Yet the construction industry also offers some evidence on how incentive programs can lead to underreporting of injuries. Contractors responding to a survey by Hinze (2005), asked why employees would not report injuries, were most likely to say, "The workers wanted to get the safety incentive associated with their incident rate," or "The workers felt pressure from other workers not to report injuries." However, this survey had a low response rate, suggesting that it may not accurately represent the construction industry or have results that generalize to other industries.

Compliance with Safety and Health Standards: OSHA Enforcement

Roughly two dozen published studies have examined the effect of OSHA inspections or enforcement of safety and health standards since OSHA was created in 1971. Some of these studies examined whether workplaces inspected early in the year had lower workday-injury rates than those inspected late in the year (Smith, 1979; McCaffrey, 1983). They typically found no other statistically significant effects of enforcement or inspection, although they also found that inspections may have had a greater effect at establishments with fewer than 100 employees (Smith, 1979). Other studies have found that more frequent inspections reduced noncompliance and that repeated inspections in particular reduced noncompliance from the first to the second inspection at an establishment (Bartel and Thomas, 1985; Weil, 2001; Gray and Jones, 2001; Ko, Mendeloff, and Gray, 2010).

Scholz and Gray (1990), in linking OSHA inspection data from 1979 to 1985 with BLS survey data, found that inspections that levied penalties were followed by a 20 percent decrease in the number of workdays lost to injuries in the subsequent two to three years.

Some studies have examined the relationship between the type of standards cited in an inspection and the subsequent change in different types of injuries. Both Mendeloff and Gray (2005) and Haviland et al. (2010) found that, among five OSHA standards examined, only inspections citing the general requirements for personal protective equipment (1910.132) helped prevent injuries. Inspections citing machine guarding (1910.212), electrical wiring (1910.0303), powered industrial trucks (1910.0178), and fire extinguisher standards (1910.0157) showed no effect on subsequent injuries.

In summary, it appears that inspections that levy penalties (which are certain if there are serious violations) are followed by substantial reductions in the rate of injuries, but these effects decay and are no longer identifiable after about two years. Some hazards surely have more effect on injuries than others, but the only clear finding is that citing PPE violations reduces injuries whereas violations of other OSHA standards show no effect on reductions in related injuries. The effects of inspections are greater at smaller workplaces (Gray and Mendeloff, 2005; Smith, 1979), perhaps because larger ones have better compliance beforehand or respond more positively to prior inspections.

Air Force inspections and compliance assessments typically occur more often than in the civilian sector, with few units going more than a year without some assessment. Nevertheless, to save costs, many visits from higher authorities or other inspection and assessment agencies have been combined, which may increase the time between evaluations and decrease compliance. The Air Force may need to revisit its scheduling of visits to ensure that they are frequent enough to maintain compliance.

A noted limitation to the above studies is that they are relatively few in number, almost all exclusive to the manufacturing sector, to measures of DART injuries, and to workplaces with more than 100 employees. We should be wary of drawing conclusions about programs based on a small number of studies. This is especially true because effects may change over time, either from changes in the regulated community or in the regulator's behavior. State worker-compensation program changes, such as increasing the ease of obtaining benefits or the size of the benefits, can also increase the number of reported injuries (Butler and Worrall, 1983; Hirsch, Macpherson, and Dumond, 1997). Other state regulation effects may also affect injury reporting. For example, Mendeloff and Burns (2012) found that, for the construction sector, states with the highest fatality rates have the lowest nonfatal injury rates, and those with the highest reported injury rates have the lowest mortality rates). Given the reliability of the fatality data, this suggests that the states reporting high fatality rates are underreporting nonfatal injuries more than other states do.

Summary

Our review included four types of practices for preventing environmental stressors. These are promoting safety culture and climate, safety training and education, financial incentives to prevent injuries, and compliance with safety regulations.

Unfortunately, there are few rigorous, high-quality studies of these practices. The reviews we cited indicate that management commitment to safety is key, particularly at high levels; safety training can affect specific, targeted behaviors; inexperienced workers are at greater risk of workplace injury; and safety inspections with penalties reduce injuries, albeit with strongest effects when inspections are related to the use of PPE. Compliance with safety standards is not always linked to a reduction in the number of injuries, but there is some evidence that inspections lead to improved compliance at the company level. There is no evidence that financial incentives improve workplace-injury rates. The Air Force can capitalize on this research by ensuring that lower-skilled Airmen are supervised and compliance inspections emphasizing PPE use are regularly scheduled.

The Air Force may wish to strengthen measures of safety culture and climate in routine climate-assessment surveys at all levels of the organization (e.g., unit and above); assess or quiz Airmen, especially junior enlisted, on their knowledge of workplace-safety procedures and reward correct knowledge; and use routine, periodic safety inspections to manage short-term compliance with safety rules and regulations. Such survey, assessment, and safety-inspection data could then be linked with exposure to environmental stressors.

In the next chapter, we discuss ways the Air Force may improve environmental fitness given that exposure may have occurred.

4. Key Resilience Factors: Protection

We now turn to protective practices that may mitigate the harmful effects of exposure to environmental stressors. We focus on PPE, acclimatization and tolerance, and ergonomics, as these have received the most attention in research and are most often the target of interventions to promote environmental fitness, as discussed in the next chapter of the report.

Personal Protective Equipment

As noted in the last chapter, Mendeloff and Gray (2005) and Haviland et al. (2010) found that the citing of manufacturing employers for violations of the PPE standard led to reduced injury rates. This OSHA standard cited in these studies (1910.132) is the one that applies generally to PPE for head, eye and face, hands, and feet, which does seem a plausible explanation for a reduced number of injuries, such as those to the eyes from grinding or welding or those to the feet from falling objects. We discuss below examples of two other types of PPE—respiratory and noise—and lessons they offer for mitigating environmental stressors. Unlike other environmental stressors, noise is one in which identifying risk exposure and prevention is of primary importance, rather than acclimatization and tolerance.

Respiratory-Protective Equipment

The value of PPE depends on its effectiveness when worn and the frequency with which it is used, as may be demonstrated by research on respiratory-protective equipment related to a separate OSHA standard (1910.134). A BLS and NIOSH (2003) survey of private-sector respiratory-protection programs found that the required use of respirators varied widely by industry, with 0.2 percent of printing firms having such a requirement, compared to 36.9 percent of chemical firms. For manufacturing as a whole, 6.7 percent of establishments required respirator use.

Unfortunately, the BLS/NIOSH survey was not able to measure exposures at the workplaces and thus was not able to determine how many establishments were, according to OSHA standards, required to provide respirators and ensure that workers wore them. In one study that compared the number of establishments cited for a respiratory-program violation to the number of establishments targeted for a health inspection, roughly one-third of all establishments requiring respirator use had some deficiency in their respiratory-protection program (Mendeloff and Kopsic, 2008). The lack of proper use indicates a potential not only for injuries but also for lost productivity and treatment expenses. From 1999 to 2006, OSHA inspectors cited respirator program violations in 12 percent of all inspections (Mendeloff et al., 2013). For OSHA health inspections (as opposed to safety inspections), the figure was 22 percent. Workplaces that receive health inspections are more likely to need respirator programs, so the latter figure may be a better indicator of the rate of noncompliance.

The most common OSHA violation was the failure to carry out proper fit-testing before requiring respirator use. Among the violations dealing with the respirator itself, the most common was the failure to evaluate the environment before choosing a respirator.

As a federal government agency, the Air Force has more stringent guidelines for the use and availability of PPE, including respiratory equipment. Given its combat mission, the military requires fit-testing of gas masks before deployment, and this information must be annotated on mobility paperwork. The same diligence should be applied to home-station PPE, such as that required when working with fuels and other potentially dangerous items or procedures.

Noise Reduction

Noise exposures can be reduced by engineering controls (e.g., sound-baffle systems), administrative controls (e.g., rotating employees out of the exposed area), and HPDs. HPDs, such as earmuffs and plugs, are considered an acceptable option with which to control exposures to noise but less desirable than effective hearing-conservation programs (Verbeek et al., 2012; U.S. Department of Labor, 2015). HPDs are less optimal because employees often report discomfort or communication problems when using them. In addition, HPDs must be properly fitted to be effective. In the military, unique situations, such as the need to also use a combat helmet or gas mask, may limit the ability to wear hearing protection comfortably—even though such situations may be those when hearing protection is most needed.

In 1983, OSHA promulgated a very detailed standard that required hearing-conservation programs at all workplaces where noise exposures exceed 85 db (*Federal Register*, 1983). Such programs include requirements for noise monitoring, baseline and annual audiograms, training, and provision of HPDs. Although OSHA has a permissible exposure limit for noise of 90 db, it adopted a policy of not requiring engineering controls unless exposures exceeded 100 db given the expense of engineering capabilities and the capability of HPDs to reduce noise exposure to less than 90 db. As a result, reliance on HPDs is very widespread, but the extent of reliance on administrative controls to reduce exposures is unknown.

DoD and the Services have had hearing-conservation programs since 1978 (GAO, 2011). In most respects, these resemble OSHA's standard. As with OSHA, DoD states that engineering controls should be the primary means of eliminating potentially harmful exposures, but the degree to which cost and feasibility issues limit the use of engineering controls is not known. The use of and adequacy of HPDs in combat situations is harder to appraise and likely to be lower. DoD observes a permissible exposure limit of 85 db rather than the OSHA limit of 90 db. Allowable exposure time is also more stringent under DoD requirements.

The military has seen longer-serving members suffer greater levels of hearing loss; more than 25 percent of those serving in the Army for more than 17 years experienced some hearing loss, compared to 5 percent of those who served less than 3 years (Smith et al., 2003).

The GAO (2011) reports that the Army's concern with hearing-related injuries in Operation Iraqi Freedom led to the requirement that soldiers who did not meet the hearing readiness standard could not be deployed. This readiness standard required up-to-date audiograms and provision of combat-arms earplugs (see also Tufts, Vasil, and Briggs, 2009). Audiograms in the Army increased from 168,000 in 2003 to almost 440,000 in 2006, largely as a result of this policy (GAO, 2011).

Yet GAO (2011) also noted some important shortcomings in the services' hearing-conservation programs. Perhaps the most important was the failure of information systems to track program implementation and effects on hearing loss. Zohar and colleagues (1980) showed that information feedback could promote use of ear protectors. More recently, NIOSH has been field-testing a device that provides real-time measurements of the actual degree of noise attenuation by HPDs (Rabinowitz et al., 2011).

Aircraft and weapon noise are two significant contributors to hearing loss in the Air Force, but some personnel may not wear hearing protection in emergency or contingency situations. One reason may be the incompatibility of HPDs with other gear, such as helmets and gas masks. The Air Force could engineer new facilities to reduce noise pollution. It can also rotate manpower so that the same personnel are not always on the shifts with the greatest amount of noise. Alternatively, it could break up shifts to reduce exposure times.

Acclimatization and Tolerance

Acclimatization is an adaptive process that reduces the physiological strain produced by constant environmental stress. *Tolerance* typically refers to the result of acclimatization at the cellular level, by which individuals adapt to and are protected from environmental stressors. *Cross-tolerance* occurs when exposing an individual to one stressor results in tolerance of other, novel environmental stressors. Measuring whether an individual has become acclimatized to a specific environmental stressor is often difficult. One way to measure acclimatization to environmental stressors is to simply ask a person if they are uncomfortable under certain conditions, such as extreme heat or high altitude (Hellon et al., 1956). Unfortunately, subjective measures of comfort or stress are highly unreliable. More recent indicators of acclimatization focus on biochemistry and cellular markers of efficient cellular performance that indicate whether acclimatization has led to heat (Horowitz, 2007) or altitude tolerance (Murray, 2009). However, such measures may be expensive and burdensome to collect from individuals routinely in real-time, outside laboratory settings. Predeployment training in the Air Force could be optimized to achieve acclimatization if the training site environmentally mimics the deployed location.

Below, we provide specific examples of how acclimatization and tolerance help protect individuals against specific physical environmental stressors caused by extreme temperature or altitude conditions.

Temperature

NIOSH (1986) has recommended the monitoring of core body temperature, skin temperature, sweat, and heart rate as appropriate indicators of heat strain. Core temperature pills (wireless transmitters ingested by subjects) to monitor heat stress may be inaccurate because of ingested fluids present when the pill is still in the upper portion of the gastrointestinal tract (Wilkinson et al., 2008). By contrast, another metric that combines two indicators is the Physiological Strain Index (PSI), developed by Moran, Shitzer, and Pandolf (1998). The PSI has demonstrated efficacy in identifying individuals with heat strain in both dry and wet environments, with or without PPE (Moran, 2000). By continuously measuring PSI to identify "at-risk" individuals, one can eliminate the need for continuous core temperature monitoring and measures that can be influenced by drinking behavior (Buller et al., 2008). The military typically identifies potentially dangerous heat conditions, temperature, and humidity combinations by tracking the wet-bulb temperature and issuing warnings as needed. Unit leaders must then institute appropriate work-rest cycles and hydration breaks while carefully monitoring those with prior heat injury,[6] Unfortunately, prior heat injury is usually known only through self-reports because medical records are not shared with deployed commanders, and deployment paperwork does not flag personnel with such history.

---

[6] For more information on hydration, see the companion report on nutritional fitness (Flórez, Shih, and Martin, 2014).

Understanding and preventing the negative effects of cold exposure is also important, although this issue has been of less concern in recent conflicts. There are currently no measures that assess resiliency to cold. Nevertheless, certain behavioral considerations, including adequate diet and fluid balance, clothing, use of PPE, and training in cold weather, can help increase acclimatization to cold and prevent injuries from it.

Altitude

Measuring whether an individual has achieved a level of tolerance for high altitudes and hypoxic conditions must be done at the cellular level. Generally, acclimatization to altitude includes some mix of exposure and recovery (Hetzler et al., 2009), although some evidence suggests that even if a standardized procedure is followed, acclimatization may still not occur (Howald and Hoppeler, 2003; Pfeiffer et al., 1999). Other research suggests that certain genetic and biological markers may indicate who is more (or less) likely to suffer from altitude-related illnesses (Friedl and Penetar, 2008; Mairbaurl et al., 2003). For example, retrospective studies that examined individuals who did and did not develop high-altitude pulmonary edema found that those who did were more likely than those who did not to have human leukocyte antigen, or HLA-DR6 and HLA-DQ4 antigens (Hanaoka et al., 1998) and differences in single nucleotide polymorphisms of the angiotensive II type 1 receptor gene (Hotta et al., 2004). Nevertheless, this research is far from conclusive in terms of using genetic markers to measure altitude resilience.

Ergonomics

Ergonomics is the study of designing equipment and devices that fit the human body, its movements, and cognitive abilities (International Ergonomics Association, 2011). The two simultaneous goals of ergonomics are to promote the health and well-being of workers and to maximize productivity. The key to accomplishing both goals is preventing injury, both short and long term. In practice, ergonomics focuses on the "fit" between individuals and the tools they need to do their jobs. For example, employees who spend hours in front of computer screens should have a workspace that reduces eye strain, provides lumbar support for the back, and allows the wrists to be straight over the keyboard. The military is known for its template approach to office work and not for its ability to ergonomically accommodate its workers. This is especially true in deployed environments.

A recent review of participatory ergonomic (PE) interventions (i.e., those in which individuals performing work must engage in problem-solving to reduce injury-related risks) found some evidence that such interventions can reduce musculoskeletal symptoms, injuries and workers' compensation claims, and days lost to injury or sickness

(Rivilis et al., 2008; Amick et al., 2006, 2009; Brewer et al., 2006). However, another recent review by Van Eerd et al. (2011) suggests that there is no one ideal approach to PE interventions, although the authors note several key elements of effective PE programs. These include use of teams to address ergonomic issues, involvement of appropriate personnel in the process (e.g., supervisors, specialists, advisors), explicit definition of participants' responsibilities (such as problem identification or solution development), use of group decisionmaking procedures, providing ergonomic training, and addressing key facilitators or barriers.

Summary

PPE, acclimatization and tolerance, and ergonomics may all mitigate the effects of environmental stressors on health and well-being. The value of PPE depends on whether it is used properly and worn at the appropriate times. Acclimatization to specific conditions, such as heat or altitude, can reduce the negative effects of exposure, but much more research is needed both to understand how that adaptation process works as well as on how to measure acclimatization. Recent reviews of workplace ergonomic programs suggest that they can reduce musculoskeletal problems, injuries and workers' compensation claims, and loss of work days to illness or injury, although the most effective ergonomic practices and policies may be job- or industry-specific. Flagging personnel with prior heat-stress injuries and ensuring that all PPE is compatible with deployment and emergency gear can also increase the Air Force's ability to protect its personnel from environmental stressors. In the next chapter, we focus on how the Air Force can use PPE to promote environmental health and the well-being of Airmen.

5. Interventions to Promote Environmental Fitness: The Role of Personal Protective Equipment

Because federal, state, and local governments, as well as private-sector firms, have focused a great deal of time and resources on establishing and validating workplace health and safety requirements, DoD and the Air Force have well-established procedures for preventing injuries and other negative outcomes related to environmental risks. Indeed, the military may have the most stringent health and injury-prevention policies and practices of all employers. From this perspective, the most important policy question becomes which interventions, besides health and safety standards, can help promote environmental health and well-being?

We suggest that appropriate use of PPE is the most promising means to prevent environmental injury. The literature on PPE use is vast and spans a variety of specific PPE used to protect individuals against specific risks in specific occupations and industries. Although this literature is informative, from a policy perspective it may be more useful to synthesize the important predictors of PPE use that span all types of equipment, jobs, and industries.

At its core, the use of PPE is about compliance. A number of researchers have developed models of human behavior change and, more specifically, of compliance (e.g., DeJoy, 1986, 1996; Gielen and Sleet, 2003; Green et al., 1980; Sulzer-Azaroff, 1987). Figure 5.1 depicts an adapted version of the model of compliance behavior proposed by McGovern et al. (2000) for health care workers.

In the model, there are three groups of determinants of compliance, or, in this example, the appropriate use of PPE. The first set of determinants is individual characteristics. These include sociodemographic characteristics (e.g., age, gender), attitudes and beliefs (e.g., about the use of safety equipment), knowledge (e.g., about the risks involved in not using safety equipment), and education (both level of attainment and on how to use safety equipment). The second set of determinants is at the job level. These include level of experience, skill, cognitive demands, workload, and work stress. The third set of determinants is at the organizational level. These include training, peer review (of safety practices), management support, and the safety culture and climate of the workplace.

Figure 5.1
Model of Determinants of Appropriate Use of PPE

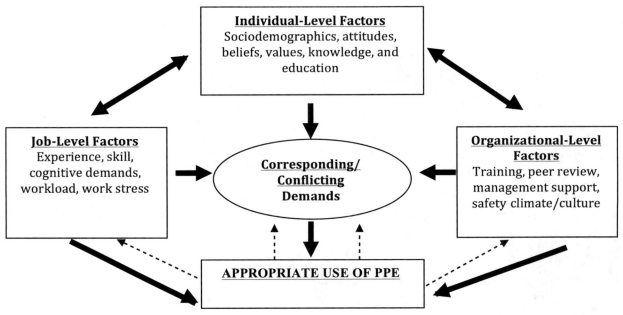

SOURCE: Adapted from McGovern et al. (2000).

Individual, job, and organizational determinants all operate in tandem to influence whether an individual chooses to use PPE, as represented by the rectangle at the bottom of Figure 5.1. For example, if an individual is aware of the risk of not using PPE, has the knowledge and skills to appropriately use PPE for a specific task, and works in an environment where management supports the use of PPE, then the likelihood of an individual appropriately using PPE is high. If the individual does not have access to appropriate PPE, does not see or is unaware of the health benefit in using PPE, or does not know how to use PPE, then the likelihood of appropriate PPE use is low. These inputs may conflict, such as when an individual is aware of the risks of not using PPE but does not do so because of possible stigmatization.

One of the most appealing aspects of this model is that it can be applied to any PPE, any environmental stressor, and any job or occupation. By contrast, the vast majority of the literature on appropriate use of PPE is industry- or job-specific. For instance, an evaluation of positive influences affecting respiratory-protective equipment use among hazardous-waste workers included concern about work exposure, fit-testing, and training, and negative ones were communication, personal comfort, effect on vision, structural environment, and fatigue (Salazar et al., 2001). Similarly, a review of 29 studies of health care worker safety that addressed the psychometric properties of "safety climate" questionnaires suggested that the most valid assessments of safety climate should include questions about positive perceptions of organizational safety (Flin et al., 2006). But at the same time, this study acknowledged that testing the validity of worker safety measures is often done by linking the measures with outcomes. In the case of health care workers, the outcome is usually both patient safety (through the worker's use of PPE) and worker injury. That may not be applicable to other industries and worker activities.

Unfortunately, at present, what the literature does not contain is any systematic overview of the results from all of these very specific studies. Thus, although the model is intuitively appealing, it has not yet led to the same rigorous interventions and evaluations that can be found in some of the other TFF domains explored in this series of documents. As such, it is important to consider both self-reported measures of PPE use and also organizational measures of safety-climate characteristics.

Regarding specific interventions to increase workplace self-protective behavior, DeJoy (1996) suggests focusing on four stages of behavior: hazard appraisal, decisionmaking, initiation, and adherence. For an individual facing an environmental stressor, or hazard, the first stage in behavior response is to *appraise the hazard*. A number of individual-level determinants depicted in the model in Figure 5.1 (e.g., attitudes, beliefs, knowledge) affect this stage. In the second stage, individuals engage in a *decisionmaking* process, weighing the costs and benefits of possible actions and assessing whether they can perform certain actions (given that self-efficacy is an important aspect of self-protective behavior).[7] In the third stage, *initiation*, environmental and organizational characteristics can support or affirm the results of the decisionmaking phase. For example, positive feedback from coworkers and managers help behavioral intentions become actual actions. In the last stage, *adherence*, both environmental and organizational, can again influence long-term compliance.

The military is in a unique position with respect to both the model of PPE use presented in Figure 5.1 and DeJoy's (1996) model. An individual's first years in the military are considered an indoctrination period, when nearly all aspects of the person's life is influenced by the organization. The Air Force is responsible for most technical training of its members and, consequently, greatly influences the initiation stage, regardless of individual background or job characteristics. Further, as long as the Air Force maintains a culture and climate of safety, with appropriate checks on compliance and high-level leadership support, its organizational characteristics should help Airmen continue to use PPE appropriately.

---

[7] For a more detailed discussion of self-efficacy, see the companion report on psychological fitness (Robson, 2014).

6. Conclusion

This report has focused on one domain of TFF, environmental fitness, which is defined as the knowledge, skills, and behaviors necessary to successfully protect against stress associated with one's environment. We identified two main constructs in which to categorize environmental fitness factors: *prevention* of exposure to environmental stressors or hazards and *protection* against environmental stressors and hazards already present in an environment.

Prevention practices include safety culture and climate, safety training and education, financial incentives to prevent injuries, and compliance with safety regulations. Unfortunately, little high-quality, rigorous research has been done on these practices. Nevertheless, the research that does exist suggests that management commitment to safety is key for workplace safety. Safety training can affect specific, targeted behaviors; and safety inspections with penalties reduce injuries, particularly in the short term and when inspections are linked to the use of PPE. There is also some evidence that inspections lead to improved compliance by companies, but compliance with safety standards is not always linked to a reduction in the number of injuries. Thus, measures of management commitment to safety and of safety inspections should focus on use of PPE and associated outcomes after program implementation.

For protective practices, we reviewed the literature on PPE, acclimatization and tolerance, and ergonomics. The value of PPE depends on whether it is used properly and worn at the appropriate times. Acclimatization to specific conditions, such as heat or altitude, can reduce the negative effects of exposure, but much more research is needed to understand how that adaptation process works. Recent reviews of workplace ergonomic programs suggest that they can be effective at preventing musculoskeletal problems, reducing injuries and workers' compensation claims, and reducing work days lost to illness or injury. Much like PPE, the ergonomic practices and policies that are most effective are often job- or industry-specific.

The Air Force has many opportunities to put to use the research reviewed in this report on environmental fitness. What should the Air Force do and measure to make sure that (1) it knows the environmental stressors Airmen face, (2) it prevents environmental stressors and exposures when possible, and (3) it protects Airmen from stressors and exposures that cannot be avoided?

First, the Air Force must decide which stressors most affect environmental fitness. We prioritized a key set of environmental stressors, including temperature (heat or cold), noise, altitude, chemicals, and workplace environments in which injuries or deaths may occur. There are numerous ways to measure exposure to these (and other environmental) stressors. Some are well established, and relatively noninvasive, inexpensive, and easy to administer or collect. Others are not. The Air Force must therefore also decide where to prioritize data-collection efforts.

Second, the Air Force may wish to focus on predictors of PPE use that cut across all types of equipment and jobs to prevent exposures of all types (not just for specific occupations and industries, which is the focus of the bulk of literature on PPE use). Compliance, and the factors that influence it, is paramount. Interventions designed to increase workplace self-protective behavior should address the various stages of behavior that affect whether an individual will use a protective device.

Third, the Air Force can target evidence-based strategies to mitigate the negative outcomes of exposure among the most relevant subgroups. For example, among young Airmen new to the military, predeployment training can help acclimatize them to deployment conditions and thereby mitigate temperature and altitude injuries. Ultimately, the Air Force should create a safety climate regarding environmental stressors. But the connection between a safety climate, where *individuals* accept the importance of safety, and a safety culture, where the *institution* is committed to safety, is very important. Workplace injuries can be reduced through a safety culture but only if both senior and mid-level leaders are visible participants and advocates.

References

Agency for Toxic Substances and Disease Registry, "Public Health Statement for Jet Fuels JP-5 and JP-8," August 2008. As of April 9, 2015: http://www.atsdr.cdc.gov/PHS/PHS.asp?id=771&tid=150

Amick, B. C., III, J. M. Tullar, S. Brewer, Q. Mahood, E. Irvin, L. Pompeii, A. Wang, D. Van Eerd, D. Gimeno, and B. Evanoff, *Interventions in Health-Care Settings to Protect Musculoskeletal Health: A Systematic Review*, Toronto, Canada: Institute for Work and Health, 2006.

Amick, B. C., III, S. Brewer, J. Tullar, D. Van Eerd, D. C. Cole, and E. Tompa, "Musculoskeletal Disorders: Examining the Best Practices for Prevention," *Professional Safety*, Vol. 54, 2009, pp. 24–28.

Azanoff, L. S., C. Levenstein, and D. H. Wegman, "Occupational Injury and Illness Surveillance: Conceptual Filters Explain Underreporting," *American Journal of Public Health*, Vol. 92, 2002, pp. 1421–1422.

B'Hymer, Clayton, Edward Krieg Jr., Kenneth L. Cheever, Christine A. Toennis, John C. Clark, James S. Kesner, Roger Gibson, and Mary Ann Butler, "Evaluation and Comparison of Urinary Metabolic Biomarkers of Exposure for the Jet Fuel JP-8," *Journal of Toxicology and Environmental Health, Part A*, Vol. 75, No. 11, 2012, pp. 661–672.

"Baker Commission Report," *The Report of the BP U.S. Refineries Independent Safety Review*, January 2007.

Bartel, A. P., and L. Glenn Thomas, "Direct and Indirect Effects of OSHA Regulation: A New Look at OSHA's Impact," *Journal of Law and Economics*, Vol. 28, 1985, pp. 1–25.

Beus, J. M., S. C. Payne, M. E. Bergman, and W. Arthur Jr., "Safety Climate and Injuries: An Examination of the Theoretical and Empirical Relationships," *Journal of Applied Psychology*, Vol. 95, 2010, pp. 713–727.

BLS—*See* U.S. Bureau of Labor Statistics.

Boden, L. I., and A. Ozonoff, "Capture-Recapture Estimates of Nonfatal Workplace Injuries and Illnesses," *Annals of Epidemiology*, Vol. 18, Issue 6, June 2008, pp. 500–506.

Boden, L. I., N. Nestoriak, and B. Pierce, "Using Capture-Recapture Analysis to Identify Factors Associated with Differential Reporting of Workplace Injuries and Illnesses," October 2010. As of June 19, 2012: www.bls.gov/osmr/pdf/st100300.pdf

Breslin, F. C., and P. Smith, "Trial by Fire: A Multivariate Examination of the Relation between Job Tenure and Work Injuries," *Occupational and Environmental Medicine*, Vol. 63, 2007, pp. 27–32.

Brewer, S., D. van Eerd, I. B. Amick, III, E. Irvin, K. M. Daum, F. Gerr, et al., "Workplace Interventions to Prevent Musculoskeletal and Visual Symptoms and Disorders Among Computer Users: A Systematic Review," *Journal of Occupational Rehabilitation*, Vol. 16, 2006, pp. 325–358.

Buller, M. J., W. A. Latzka, M. Yokota, W. J. Tharion, and D. S. Moran, "A Real-Time Heat Strain Risk Classifier Using Heart Rate and Skin Temperature," *Physiological Measures*, Vol. 29, 2008, pp. N79–N85.

Butler, R. J., and J. D. Worrall, "Workers' Compensation: Benefits and Injury Claims Rates in the Seventies," *Review of Economics and Statistics*, Vol. 65, No. 4, 1983, pp. 580–589.

Chao, Yi-Chun E., Roger L. Gibson, and Leena A. Nylander-French, "Dermal Exposure to Jet Fuel (JP-8) in US Air Force Personnel," *The Annals of Occupational Hygiene*, Vol. 49, No. 7, October 2005, pp. 639–645.

Chao, Yi-Chun E., Lawrence L. Kupper, Berrin Serdar, Peter P. Egeghy, Stephen M. Rappaport, and Leena A. Nylander-French, "Dermal Exposure to Jet Fuel JP-8 Significantly Contributes to the Production of Urinary Naphthols in Fuel-Cell Maintenance Workers," *Environmental Health Perspectives*, Vol. 114, No. 2, February 2006, pp. 182–185.

Clarke, S. G., "Safety Culture: Under-Specified and Overrated?" *International Journal of Management Reviews*, Vol. 2, 2000, pp. 65–90.

DCoE—*See* Defense Centers of Excellence for Psychological Health and Traumatic Brain Injury.

Defense Centers of Excellence for Psychological Health and Traumatic Brain Injury, 2011. As of April 9, 2011:
http://www.dcoe.health.mil/

DeJoy, D. M., "A Behavioral Diagnostic Model for Self-Protective Behavior in the Workplace," *Professional Safety*, December 1986, pp. 26–30.

———, "Theoretical Models of Health Behavior and Workplace Self-Protective Behavior," *Journal of Safety Research*, Vol. 26, 1996, pp. 61–72.

Doll, R., and R. Peto, "The Causes of Cancer: Quantitative Estimates of Avoidable Risks of Cancer in the United States Today," *Journal of the National Cancer Institute*, Vol. 66, 1981, pp. 1191–1308.

Federal Register, Final Rule: OSHA Hearing Conservation Standard, March 8, 1983, pp. 9738–9784.

Flin, R., C. Burns, K. Mearns, S. Yule, and E. M. Robertson, "Measuring Safety Climate in Health Care," *Quality and Safety in Health Care*, Vol, 15, No. 2, April 2006, pp. 109–115.

Flórez, Karen R., Regina A. Shih, and Margret T. Martin, *Nutritional Fitness and Resilience: A Review of Relevant Constructs, Measures, and Links to Well-Being*, Santa Monica, Calif.: RAND Corporation, RR-105-AF, 2014. As of March 27, 2015: http://www.rand.org/pubs/research_reports/RR105.html

Freeman, D., M. Gittins, K. Pugh, A. Antley, M. Slater, and G. Dunn, "What Makes One Person Paranoid and Another Person Anxious? The Differential Prediction of Social Anxiety and Persecutory Ideation in an Experimental Situation," *Psychological Medicine*, Vol. 38, No. 8, August 2008, pp. 1121–1132.

Friedl, K. E., and D. M. Penetar, "Resilience and Survival in Extreme Environments," in V. Tepe and B. J. Lukey (eds.), *Biobehavioral Resilience to Stress*, Cleveland, Ohio: CRC Press, 2008, pp. 139–176.

Frisancho, R. A., "Acclimation and Acclimatization to Hot Climates: Native and Nonnative Populations," in *Human Adaptation and Accommodation*, Ann Arbor, Mich.: University of Michigan Press, 1993, pp. 53–77.

GAO—*See* U.S. Government Accountability Office.

Gielen, A. C., and D. Sleet, "Application of Behavior-Change Theories and Methods to Injury Prevention," *Epidemiologic Reviews*, Vol. 25, 2003, pp. 65–76.

Givoni B., and R. F. Goldman, "Predicting Rectal Temperature Response to Work, Environment, and Clothing," *Journal of Applied Physiology*, Vol. 32, 1972, pp. 812–822.

Gray, W. B., and C. Adaire Jones, "Longitudinal Patterns of Compliance with OSHA in the Manufacturing Sector," *Journal of Human Resources*, Fall 1991, pp. 623–653.

Gray, W. B., and J. Mendeloff, "The Declining Effects of OSHA Inspections in Manufacturing, 1979–1998," *Industrial and Labor Relations Review*, Vol. 58, 2005, pp. 571–587.

Green, L. W., M. W. Kreuter, S. G. Deeds, and K. B. Partridge, *Health Education Planning: A Diagnostic Approach*, Palo Alto, Calif.: Mayfield, 1980.

Hanaoka, M., K. Kubo, Y. Yamazaki, T. Mihahara, Y. Matsuzawa, T. Kobayashi, et al., "Association of High-Altitude Pulmonary Edema with the Major Histocompatability Complex," *Circulation*, Vol. 97, 1998, pp. 1124–1128.

Haviland, A., R. Burns, W. Gray, T. Ruder, and J. Mendeloff, *The Impact of OSHA Inspections on Lost Time Injuries in Manufacturing: Pennsylvania Manufacturing, 1998–2005*, Santa Monica, Calif.: RAND Corporation, WR-592-PA, 2008.

Haviland, A., R. Burns, W. Gray, T. Ruder, and J. Mendeloff, "What Kinds of Injuries Do OSHA Inspections Prevent?" *Journal of Safety Research*, Vol. 41, 2010, pp. 339–345.

Hellon, R. F., R. M. Jones, R. K. Macpherson, and J. S. Weiner, "Natural and Artificial Acclimatization to Hot Environments," *Journal of Physiology*, Vol. 132, 1956, pp. 559–576.

Hetzler, R. K., C. D. Stickley, I. F. Kimura, M. LaBotz, A. W. Nichols, K. T. Nakasone, R. W. Sargent, and L. P. A. Burgess, "The Effect of Dynamic Intermittent Hypoxic Conditioning on Arterial Oxygen Saturation," *Wilderness and Environmental Medicine*, Vol. 20, 2009, pp. 26–32.

Hinze J., *Injury Under-Reporting in the United States Construction Industry*, Gainesville, Fl.: M. E. Rinker, Sr. School of Building Construction, University of Florida, 2005. As of June 19, 2012:
http://web.dcp.ufl.edu/hinze/Under-Reporting-Final-Report.htm

Hirsch, B. T., D. A. Macpherson, and J. M. Dumond, ''Workers' Compensation Recipiency in Union and Nonunion Workplaces,'' *Industrial and Labor Relations Review*, Vol. 50, No. 2, 1997, pp. 213–236.

Horowitz, M. "Heat Acclimation and Cross-Tolerance Against Novel Stressors: Genomic-Physiological Linkage," *Progress in Brain Research*, Vol. 162, 2007, pp. 373–392.

Hotta, J., M. Hanaoka, Y. Droma, Y. Katsuyama, M. Ota, and T. Kobayashi, "Polymorphisms of Rennin-Angiotensin System Genes with High-Altitude Pulmonary Edema in Japanese Subjects," *Chest*, Vol. 126, 2004, pp. 825–830.

Howald, H., and H. Hoppeler, "Performing at Extreme Altitude: Muscle Cellular and Subcellular Adaptations," *European Journal of Applied Physiology*, Vol. 90, 2003, pp. 360–364.

Humes, L. E., L. M. Joellenback, and J. S. Durch (eds.), *Noise and Military Service: Implications for Hearing Loss and Tinnitus*, Washington, D.C.: National Academy Press, 2005.

Institute for Work and Health, *Benchmarking Organizational Leading Indicators for the Prevention and Management of Injuries and Illnesses: Final Report*, Toronto, Canada, January 2011. As of June 19, 2012:
http://www.iwh.on.ca/benchmarking-organizational-leading-indicators

International Ergonomics Association, "What Is Ergonomics?" online, last updated November 28, 2011. As of June 19, 2012:
http://iea.cc/01_what/What%20is%20Ergonomics.html

Ko, K., J. Mendeloff, and W. Gray, "The Effect of Inspection Sequence on Non-Compliance Found in OSHA Inspections," *Regulation and Governance*, Vol. 4, 2010, pp. 48–70.

LaTourrette, Tom, and John Mendeloff, *Mandatory Workplace Safety and Health Programs: Implementation, Effectiveness, and Benefit-Cost Trade-Offs*, Santa Monica, Calif.: RAND Corporation, TR-604-PA, 2008. As of June 10, 2015:
http://www.rand.org/pubs/technical_reports/TR604

Lounsbury, D. E. (ed.), "Textbook of Military Medicine," Washington, D.C.: Office of the Surgeon General, Department of the Army, 2003.

Mairbaurl, H., F. Schwobel, S. Hoschele, M. Maggiornini, S. Gibbs, E. R. Swenson, and P. Bartsch, "Altered Ion Transporter Expression in Bronchial Epithelium in Mountaineers with High-Altitude Pulmonary Edema," *Journal of Applied Physiology*, Vol. 95, 2003, pp. 1843–1850.

Maule, Alexis L., Kristin J. Heaton, Ema Rodrigues, Kristen W. Smith, Michael D. McClean, and Susan P. Proctor, "Postural Sway and Exposure to Jet Propulsion Fuel 8 Among Us Air Force Personnel," *Journal of Occupational and Environmental Medicine*, Vol. 55, No. 4, April 2013, pp. 446–453.

May, L. M., C. Weese, D. L. Ashley, D. H. Trump, C. M. Bowling, and A. P. Lee, "The Recommended Role of Exposure Biomarkers for the Surveillance of Environmental and Occupational Chemical Exposures in Military Deployments: Policy Considerations," *Military Medicine*, Vol. 169, 2004, pp. 761–767.

McCaffrey, D. P., "An Assessment of OSHA's Recent Effects on Injury Rates," *Journal of Human Resources*, Vol. 18, 1983, pp. 131–46.

McGene, Juliana, *Social Fitness and Resilience: A Review of Relevant Constructs, Measures, and Links to Well-Being*, Santa Monica, Calif.: RAND Corporation, RR-108-AF, 2013. As of March 27, 2015:
http://www.rand.org/pubs/research_reports/RR108.html

McGovern, P. M., D. Vesley, L. Kochevar, R. R. M. Gershon, F. S. Rhame, and E. Anderson, "Factors Affecting Universal Precautions Compliance," *Journal of Business and Psychology*, Vol. 15, 2000, pp. 149–161.

Meadows, Sarah O., Laura L. Miller, and Sean Robson, *Airman and Family Resilience: Lessons from the Scientific Literature*, Santa Monica, Calif.: RAND Corporation, RR-106-AF, 2015.

Mendeloff, J., and W. B. Gray, "Inside the Black Box: How Do OSHA Inspections Lead to Reductions in Injuries?" *Law and Policy*, Vol. 27, 2005, pp. 219–237.

Mendeloff, J., and J. Kopsic, *Using OSHA Inspection Data for Surveillance of the Use and Misuse of Personal Protective Equipment*, Report to the National Personal Protection

Technology Laboratory, Washington, D.C.: National Institute for Occupational Safety and Health, 2008.

Mendeloff, J., and R. Burns, "States with Low Non-Fatal Injury Rates Have High Fatality Rates and Vice-Versa," *American Journal of Industrial Medicine*, 2012.

Mendeloff, J., C. Nelson, K. Ko, and A. Haviland, *Small Businesses and Workplace Fatality Risk: An Exploratory Analysis*, Santa Monica, Calif.: RAND Corporation, TR-371-ICJ, 2006. As of June 19, 2012:
http://www.rand.org/pubs/technical_reports/TR371.html

Mendeloff, J., R. Burns, X. Fan, J. Kopsic, and J. Xia, "Is Louisiana Really the Safest State? Comparing Fatal and Non-Fatal Injury Rates in Construction," forthcoming.

Mendeloff, John, Maryann D'Alessandro, Hangsheng Liu, Jessica Kopsic, Elizabeth Steiner, and Rachel Burns, "Using OSHA Inspection Data to Analyze Respirator Protection," *Monthly Labor Review*, December 2013.

Merchant-Borna, Kian, Ema G. Rodrigues, Kristen W. Smith, Susan P. Proctor, and Michael D. McClean, "Characterization of Inhalation Exposure to Jet Fuel Among U.S. Air Force Personnel," *The Annals of Occupational Hygiene*, Vol. 56, No. 6, July 2011, pp. 746–745.

Middendorf, P. J., "Surveillance of Occupational Noise Exposures Using OSHA's Integrated Management Information System," *American Journal of Industrial Medicine*, Vol. 46, 2004, pp. 492–504.

Moran, D. S., "Stress Evaluation by the Physiological Strain Index (PSI)," *Journal of Basic and Clinical Physiology and Pharmacology*, Vol. 11, 2000, pp. 403–423.

Moran, D. S., A. Shitzer, and K. B. Pandolf, "A Physiological Strain Index to Evaluate Heat Stress," *American Journal of Physiology*, Vol. 275, 1998, pp. R129–R134.

Mullen, Admiral Michael, "On Total Force Fitness in War and Peace," *Military Medicine*, Vol. 175, Supplement 2010, pp. 1–2.

Murray, Andrew J., "Metabolic Adaptation of Skeletal Muscle to High Altitude Hypoxia: How New Technologies Could Resolve the Controversies," *Genome Medicine*, Vol. 1, No. 12, Article 117, December 2009. As of March 30, 2015:
http://www.biomedcentral.com/content/pdf/gm117.pdf

Muza, S. R., L. E. Banderet, and B. Cadarette, "Protective Uniforms for Nuclear, Biological and Chemical Warfare," in K. B. Pandolf and R. E. Burr (eds.), *Medical Aspects of Harsh Environments*, Falls Church, Va.: Office of the Surgeon General, United States Army, Chapter 36, 2001, pp. 1084–1127.

National Institute for Occupational Safety and Health, *Criteria for a Recommended Standard: Occupational Exposure to Hot Environment*, Washington, D.C., Publication #86-113, 1986, pp. 101–110.

National Safety Council, *Workplace Employee Perception Surveys.* As of September 13, 2011: http://www.nsc.org/safety_work/Documents/Survey%20Info%20Pack%20-%20revised%202009.pdf

NIOSH—*See* National Institute for Occupational Safety and Health.

O'Conner, F. G., P. A. Deuster, D. W. DeGroot, and D. W. White, "Medical and Environmental Fitness," *Military Medicine*, Vol. 175 (August Supplement), 2010, pp. 57–64.

Occupational Safety and Health Administration, "Review of the Literature on Safety Incentives," Docket No-S-777 Ex.502-281, Washington, D.C., 1998.

OSHA—*See* Occupational Safety and Health Administration.

Palmer, K. T., M. J. Griffin, H. E. Syddall, A. Davis, B. Pannett, and D. Coggon, "Occupational Exposure to Noise and the Attributable Burden of Hearing Difficulties in Great Britain," *Occupational and Environmental Medicine*, Vol. 59, 2002, pp. 634–639.

Pleil, Joachim D., Leslie B. Smith, and Sanford D. Zelnick, "Personal Exposure to JP-8 Jet Fuel Vapors and Exhaust at Air Force Bases," *Environmental Health Perspectives*, Vol. 108, No. 3, March 2000, pp. 183–192.

Pfeiffer, J. M., E. W. Askew, E. E. Roberts, S. M. Wood, J. E. Benson, S. C. Johnson, and M. S. Freedman, "Effect of Antioxidant Supplementation on Urine and Blood Markers of Oxidative Stress During Extended Moderate-Altitude Training," *Wilderness and Environmental Medicine*, Vol. 10, 1999, pp. 66–74.

Pidgeon, N. F., "The Limits to Safety Culture: Politics, Learning and Man-Made Disasters," *Journal of Continuing Crisis Management*, Vol. 5, 1997, pp. 1–14.

Proctor, Susan P., Kristin J. Heaton, Kristen W. Smith, Ema R. Rodrigues, Drew E. Eiding, Robert Herrick, Jennifer J. Vasterling, and Michael D. McClean, "The Occupational JP8 Exposure Neuroepidemiology Study (OJENES): Repeated Workday Exposure and Central Nervous System Functioning Among US Air Force Personnel," *NeuroToxicology*, Vol. 32, No. 6, December 2011, pp. 799–808.

Rabinowitz, P. M., D. Galusha, S. R., Kirsche, M. R. Cullen, M. D. Slade, and C. Dixon-Ernst, "Effect of Daily Noise Exposure Monitoring on Annual Rates of Hearing Loss in Industrial Workers," *Occupational and Environmental Medicine*, Vol. 68, 2011, pp. 414–418.

Ritenour, A. E., A. Wickley, J. S., Ritenour, B. R. Kriete, L. H. Blackbourne, J. B. Holcomb, and C. E. Wade, "Tympanic Membrane Perforation and Hearing Loss From Blast Overpressure in Operation Enduring Freedom and Operation Iraqi Freedom Wounded," *Trauma*, Vol. 64, 2008, pp. S174–S178.

Rivilis, I., D. Van Eerd, K. Cullen, D. C. Cole, E. Irvin, J. Tyson, et al., "Effectiveness of Participatory Ergonomic Interventions on Health Outcomes: A Systematic Review," *Applied Ergonomics*, Vol. 39, 2008, pp. 342–358.

Robson L., C. Stephenson, P. Schulte, B. Amick, S. Chan, A. Bielecky, A. Wang, T. Heidotting, E. Irvin, D. Eggerth, R. Peters J. Clarke, K. Cullen, L. Boldt, C. Rotunda, and P. Grubb, *A Systematic Review of the Effectiveness of Training & Education for the Protection of Workers*, Toronto, Canada: Institute for Work and Health, January 2010; Cincinnati, Ohio: NIOSH, Publication No. 2010-127. As of June 19, 2012:
http://www.cdc.gov/niosh/docs/2010-127/pdfs/2010-127.pdf

Robson, Sean, *Physical Fitness and Resilience: A Review of Relevant Constructs, Measures, and Links to Well-Being*, Santa Monica, Calif.: RAND Corporation, RR-104-AF, 2013. As of March 27, 2015:
http://www.rand.org/pubs/research_reports/RR104.html

Robson, Sean, *Psychological Fitness and Resilience: A Review of Relevant Constructs, Measures, and Links to Well-Being*, Santa Monica, Calif.: RAND Corporation, RR-102-AF, 2014. As of March 27, 2015:
http://www.rand.org/pubs/research_reports/RR102.html

Robson, Sean, and Nicholas Salcedo, *Behavioral Fitness and Resilience: A Review of Relevant Constructs, Measures, and Links to Well-Being*, Santa Monica, Calif.: RAND Corporation, RR-103-AF, 2014. As of March 27, 2015:
http://www.rand.org/pubs/research_reports/RR103.html

Rock, P. B., "Mountains and Military Medicine: An Overview," in. P. B., Rock (ed.), *Medical Aspects of Harsh Environments. Vol. 2. Section III: Mountain Environments,* Washington, D.C.: Borden Institute, Walter Reed Army Medical Center, 2002.

Rushton, L., S. Bagga, R. Bevan, et al., "Occupation and Cancer in Britain," *British Journal of Cancer*, Vol. 102, 2010, pp. 1428–1437.

Salazar, Mary K., Catherine Connon, Timothy K. Takaro, Nancy Beaudet, and Scott Barnhart, "An Evaluation of Factors Affecting Hazardous Waste Workers' Use of Respiratory Protective Equipment," *AIHA Journal*, Vol. 62, No. 2, 2001, pp. 236–245.

Scholz, J., and W. B. Gray, "OSHA Enforcement and Workplace Injuries: A Behavioral Approach to Risk Assessment," *Journal of Risk and Uncertainty*, Vol. 3, 1990, pp. 283–305.

Serdar, Berrin, Peter P. Egeghy, Suramya Waidyanatha, Roger Gibson, and Stephen M. Rappaport, "Urinary Biomarkers of Exposure to Jet Fuel (JP-8)," *Environmental Health Perspectives*, Vol. 111, No. 14, November 2003, pp. 1760-1764.

Serra, C., M. C. Rodriquez, G. L. Delclos, M. Plana, L. I. Gomez Lopes, and F. G. Benavides, "Criteria and Methods Used for the Assessment of Fitness for Work: A Systematic Review," *Occupational Environment and Medicine*, Vol. 64, 2007, pp. 304-312.

Shih, Regina A., Sarah O. Meadows, and Margret T. Martin, *Medical Fitness and Resilience: A Review of Relevant Constructs, Measures, and Links to Well-Being*, Santa Monica, Calif.: RAND Corporation, RR-107-AF, 2013. As of March 27, 2015: http://www.rand.org/pubs/research_reports/RR107.html

Shih, Regina A., Sarah O. Meadows, John Mendeloff, and Kirby Bowling, *Environmental Fitness and Resilience: A Review of Relevant Constructs, Measures, and Links to Well-Being*, Santa Monica, Calif.: RAND Corporation, RR-101-AF, 2015.

Smith, D. L., T. S. Manning, and S. J. Petruzzello, "Effect of Strenuous Live-Fire Drills on Cardiovascular and Psychological Responses of Recruit Fire Fighters," *Ergonomics*, Vol. 44, 2001, pp. 244–254.

Smith, Kristen W., Susan P. Proctor, Al Ozonoff, and Michael D. McClean, "Inhalation Exposure to Jet Fuel (JP8) Among U.S. Air Force Personnel," *Journal of Occupational and Environmental Hygiene*, Vol. 7, No. 10, October 2010, pp. 563–572.

Smith, Kristen W., Susan P. Proctor, A. L. Ozonoff, and Michael D. McClean, "Urinary Biomarkers of Occupational Jet Fuel Exposure Among Air Force Personnel," *Journal of Exposure Science and Environmental Epidemiology*, Vol. 22, No. 1, January 2012, pp. 35–45.

Smith, P.D., D. Ohlin, S. Smith, and W. Rice, "Selected Topics In Deployment Occupational Medicine," in W.P. Kelley (ed.), *Military Preventive Medicine: Mobilization and Deployment, Vol. 1*, Washington, D.C.; Borden Institute, Walter Reed Army Medical Center, 2003.

Smith, R. S., "The Impact of OSHA Inspections of Manufacturing Injury Rates," *Journal of Human Resources*, Vol. 14, 1979, pp. 145–170.

Sulzer-Azaroff, B., "The Modification of Occupational Safety Behavior," *Journal of Occupational Accidents*, Vol. 9, 1987, pp. 177–197.

Suter, A. H., "Development of Standards and Regulations for Occupational Noise," in M. J. Crocker (ed.), *Handbook of Noise and Vibration Control*, Hoboken, N.J.: John Wiley and Sons, Inc., 2008.

Tak, S., R. R. Davis, G.M. Calvert, "Exposure to Hazardous Workplace Noice and Use of Hearing Protection Devises Among US Workers—NHANES, 1999–2004," *American Journal of Industrial Medicine*, Vol. 52, No. 5, 2009, pp. 359–371.

Tu, Raymond H., Clifford S. Mitchell, Gary G. Kay, and Terence H. Risby, "Human Exposure to the Jet Fuel, JP-8," *Aviation, Space, and Environmental Medicine*, Vol. 75, No. 1, January 2004, pp. 49–59.

Tufts, J. B., K. A. Vasil, and L. Briggs, "Auditory Fitness for Duty: A Review," *Journal of the American Academy of Audiology*, Vol. 20, 2009, pp. 539–557.

U.S. Army, "Heat Related Injuries, U.S. Army, 2005," *MSMR Medical Surveillance Monthly Report*, Vol. 12, 2006. As of September 14, 2011:
http://amsa.army.mil

U.S. Bureau of Labor Statistics, *Survey of Occupational Injuries and Illnesses*, 2009.

U.S. Bureau of Labor Statistics, *Census of Fatal Occupational Injuries: Occupation by Event or Exposure,* 2012. As of April 9, 2015:
http://www.bls.gov/iif/oshwc/cfoi/cftb0272.pdf

U.S. Bureau of Labor Statistics and National Institute of Occupational Safety and Health, *Respirator Usage in Private Sector Firms, 2001*, U.S. Department of Labor, Bureau of Labor Statistics/U.S. Department of Health and Human Services, Public Health Service, Centers for Disease Control and Prevention, National Institute for Occupational Safety and Health, 2003.

U.S. Department of Labor, Occupational Safety & Health Administration, *Occupational Noise Exposure*, 2015. As of April 10, 2015:
https://www.osha.gov/SLTC/noisehearingconservation/

U.S. Government Accountability Office, *Hearing Loss Prevention: Improvements to DOD Hearing Conservation Programs Could Lead to Better Outcomes*, Washington, D.C., GAO-11-114, January 2011. As of June 19, 2012:
http://www.gao.gov/new.items/d11114.pdf

U.S. House Committee on Transportation and Infrastructure, "The Impact of Railroad Injury, Accident, and Discipline Policies on the Safety of America's Railroads," October 25, 2007. As of March 30, 2015:
http://www.gpo.gov/fdsys/pkg/CHRG-110hhrg38568/html/CHRG-110hhrg38568.htm

Van Eerd, D., D. Cole, E. Irvin, Q. Mahood, K. Keown, N. Theberge, J. Village, M. St. Vincent, and K. Cullen, "Process and Implementation of Participatory Ergonomic Interventions: A Systematic Review," *Ergonomics*, Vol. 53, 2011, pp. 1153–1166.

Verbeek, J. H., E. Kateman, C. Morata, W. A. Dreschler, and C. Mischke, "Interventions to Prevent Occupational Noise-Inducing Hearing Loss," *Cochrane Database of Systematic*

Reviews, 2012. As of April 10, 2015:
http://onlinelibrary.wiley.com/doi/10.1002/14651858.CD006396.pub3/full

Weil, D., "Assessing OSHA's Performance: New Evidence from the Construction Industry," *Journal of Policy Analysis and Management*, Vol. 20, 2001, pp. 651–674.

Wilkinson, D. M., J. M. Carter, V. L. Richmond, S. D. Blacker, and M. P. Rayson, "The Effect of Cool Water Ingestion on Gastrointestinal Pill Temperature," *Medicine and Science in Sports and Exercise*, Vol. 40, 2008, pp. 523–528.

Wright-Patterson Air Force Base, "Voluntary Protection Program," undated. As of March 30, 2015:
http://www.wpafb.af.mil/units/vpp/

Yeung, Douglas, and Margret T. Martin, *Spiritual Fitness and Resilience: A Review of Relevant Constructs, Measures, and Links to Well-Being*, Santa Monica, Calif.: RAND Corporation, RR-100-AF, 2013. As of March 27, 2015:
http://www.rand.org/pubs/research_reports/RR100.html

Zimbardo, Philip G., Susan M. Andersen, and Loren G. Kabat, "Induced Hearing Deficit Generates Experimental Paranoia," *Science*, Vol. 212, No. 4502, June 26, 1981, pp. 1529–1531.

Zohar, D., "Safety Climate in Industrial Organizations: Theoretical and Applied Implications," *Journal of Applied Psychology*, Vol. 65, 1980, pp. 96–102.

_____, "Thirty Years of Safety Climate Research: Reflections and Future Directions," *Accident Analysis and Prevention*, Vol. 42, 2010, pp. 1517–1522.

Zohar, D., A. Cohen, and N. Azar, "Promoting Increased Use of Ear Protectors in Noise Through Information Feedback," *Human Factors: The Journal of the Human Factors and Ergonomics Society*, Vol. 22, 1980, pp. 69–79.